RECOGNITION

MR LISP.

ISBN 978-1-3999-3356-8

MR LISP.

Acknowledgements

I would like to take this opportunity to give acknowledgements and thanks to everyone, who genuinely believed in me, encouraged me, and kept me on track when I felt like giving up.

Everyone who pushed me to fulfill my goals, dreams, and aspirations, sat and spent time giving me constructive criticism, sound advice, and listening to my views and opinions.

I would like to extend an extra thank you (*not in chronological order*) to my mum (Winnie) and dad (Ricky) for absolutely everything, my sisters (Chantelle, Deyon, and Cassandra) for ongoing encouragement, my partner (Marie) for guidance, continuous support, and understanding, Little Joe who is a long-time family friend who has shown me nothing but support, guidance, and wisdom throughout my life. My good friend T'kisha George, who has been inspirational and has kept me highly motivated, sound, and balanced (more than she actually knows).

A special thank you to Leslie-Ann for the continuous support and guidance.

Shout out to Koaq (CEO of Triiiple I Music) for the support and for pushing me out of my comfort zone, enabling me to develop and grow.

A special shout out to Sabrina Hippolyte-Rogers (my managing agent), my aunty Mandella Briscoe, Elisha Carter *@Thecherrymoonlondon*

Acknowledgements

Caroline Boseley @*studio_west_gallery*, Jermall Blake @*jbfitformulauk* and my sister-in-law Kriss-tina.

A special thank you to my children (Reshayne, Tashay, and Shae-ana.) My biggest inspirations and without them this wouldn't be possible.

I know the list is endless, so no hard feelings to anyone who may have not been directly mentioned, just know the appreciation and gratitude is there and will always be there.

I dedicate this book in loving memory of Tiernan and Teegan Bailey, gone but never forgotten, sleep in eternal peace until we meet again.

Daddy loves you xxx

SPOKENWORD /POETRY

CONTENTS

SPOKENWORD /POETRY

CONTENTS

....

" IT'S NOT MY JOB TO CHANGE YOU, IT'S TO EMPOWER AND SUPPORT YOU TO BE THE BEST YOU CAN BE, SO IT BEGINS WITH YOU NOT WITH ME "
MR LISP 2022

RECOGNITION

Recognition

/rɛkəgˈnɪʃ(ə)n/

Learn to pronounce

noun

1. 1.

    identification of someone or something or person from previous encounters or knowledge.

    "she saw him pass by without a sign of recognition"

    Similar:

    identification

    recall

    remembrance

2. 2.

    acknowledgement of the existence, validity, or legality of something.

    "The unions must receive proper recognition"

    Similar:

    acknowledgement

acceptance

admission

conceding

concession

granting

realization

Definition from Oxford Languages

WHAT IS YOUR DEFINITION OF THE WORD RECOGNITION?

_____

_____

_____

_____

_____

_____

_____

MY DEFINITION OF THE WORD RECOGNITION

Recognition to me is more than a word, it's a feeling, something we all can relate to, have you ever had that penny drop feeling? The identification within yourself and others, the understanding, the moment things start to make sense, have you ever seen someone and can't put the name to a face or a place of knowing?

It can leave you feeling frustrated, exhausted, and confused, but when the coordinates start to align and you recall who, when, and where, that feeling of being able to exhale, move forward, and progress with your activities…. that's **RECOGNITION.**

Recognition to me is that unique feeling, if you could capture that feeling and inject it throughout your life, filling all those lost, time-consumed moments of uncertainty, doubt, confusion, and lack of direction. You would be able to focus on moving forward, a deeper understanding of yourself, life, and decisions.

Recognition comes from what is inside and you have to let it out, sometimes we relate recognition based on what others see in us and we look for approval. The question we have to ask ourselves is whether the person or people showing you recognition are their views and opinions really valid? And why do we accept recognition from some people but not all?

As humans, we constantly strive for recognition and validation from others, who we deem credible, but due to our own personal situations and life experiences our judgment can be off or biased and this is where self-recognition becomes vital.

If we cannot relate to or identify within ourselves, we can end up pursuing social acceptance from others to fit in, belong or become part of a collective, without any or minimal, personal satisfaction, gratification, or desire.

How many times have you heard "You should go for that job, you would be perfect for that role" "You two should be together you will be a lovely couple" "You have the ability to change him or her" and many times we pursue things as others have suggested or highlighted it to us.

 A key note to remember is not everyone has your best interest at heart (*not stating that some individuals do not*) but only you know the true you.

So do what's going to make you happy, give you self-belief, and overall benefit yourself, instead of making decisions to appease others and give them self-gratification. That being said, sometimes it does take others to push and encourage you or help you to identify within yourself.

Overall, you have to be self-aware, have self-belief and recognition within yourself to understand who you are, what you want, what you stand for, and what you bring to the table, as we all bring something.

RECOGNITION

When the penny drops it's a feeling like no other, like picking up a Tuppa-ware dish and instantly finding the right cover.
I know you can relate, deep down that feeling feels, OOOOOHHHHH so great.
those small moments of satisfaction, that empower you to continue with your forward action.
Recognition is such a dominant word, misinterpreted, and can be confused by what is known and heard.
I remember you, you remember me, that's recognition of the faces we see.
Those songs that we hear, that bring you back to a year, that's recognition by sound to your ears.
Recognition is how we develop and learn, what information we store and what is reprocessed and churned.
Pins, passwords, fingerprints, and face ID, this is digital recognition by technology.
Inner confidence, drive, and determination to succeed and it's time we take recognition in our true abilities.
There is recognition in you and there is recognition in me, so without recognition who are we? Who are we?

WRITTEN BY
MR LISP

(This piece was written to express and create an understanding of the word recognition and the importance of recognition and not to dismiss recognition within yourself

and your attributes, as everyone brings something to the table it's just about identifying what you bring, and with understanding what you bring, you have the ability to make more conscious decisions.)

" EVERYONE BRINGS SOMETHING TO THE TABLE, IT'S JUST ABOUT IDENTIFYING WHAT YOU BRING"

MR LISP 2022

My name is Nathanael Bailey aka Mr. Lisp on the account I have a speech impediment (lisp). I have difficulties pronouncing the letter S, growing up I've always known I didn't sound like everyone else *(which I never embraced)* a uniqueness so pure, if I knew what I had, the opportunities I would have seized. *(Hindsight is such a wonderful thing.)* but it's my time now to go access my dreams.

I have had numerous jobs in different fields that have helped shape me to become the man that I am, I have a counselling background specialising in cognitive behavioural therapy, substance misuse, and offending behaviour.

I decided to compile some of my spoken words into a book to help inspire others to change or develop their thought process and find their inner being, regardless of personal situations you can prevail to great heights.

If I can do it, anyone can, you just have to believe in yourself and be prepared to look at life from a different perspective, or sometimes someone else's perspective.

If you want more out of life and desire to be a bigger and better version of yourself this book may be a great help to your development, growth, and self-confidence.

This book is not a bible or accredited by any awarding bodies (any organisation or awarding bodies wanting to accredit please get in contact.)

This book is based around cognitive behavioral therapy and problem-based solutions with a twist. It is inspired by spoken word/poetry (I recommend you read these more than once at different times of your journey as there are some strategically placed gems that will stimulate your thought process, emotions and self-development.

I believe channeling our thoughts and emotions onto paper gives us a platform to address and express ourselves and possibly be able to support others who may be experiencing similar situations.

I believe spoken word/poetry is art, and art is a form of psychotherapy that is a fundamental method for expression and communication.

I've always dreamed of writing and publishing a book, and I guess it's no longer a dream it's reality, I'm a firm believer in seizing an opportunity, being the best that you can be, and fully indulging within your own inner confidence till it oozes out of your pores and misinterpreted with arrogance and cockiness.

Sometimes we just have to big up ourselves, as throughout life I've learnt if you don't put yourself on a pedal stool not many people will.

We all want to be successful, but ask yourself, how many people want you to be successful? and how do you measure success?

SHE SELLS, SEASHELLS BY THE SEASHORE

I used to be an individual that found it so hard to speak, but now I'll advocate for the hard-to-reach.

If you can relate to my struggle then empathize with my pain, to have a thesaurus of words that just won't leave your brain, sometimes you struggle just to say your name.

Take a deep breath…….. and start again, some people stammer aka stutter, wishing the words could spread like butter.

I have a lisp and I can't pronounce "S" back in the day, it caused me nothing but stress.

Going through puberty I discovered breasts, my testicles dropped! I found hairs on my chest! my voice had broken but I still couldn't pronounce "S" FRUSTRATED.

I was frequently teased, till the point, I started to appease say "She sells seashells by the sea shore" on a regular basis, this is what I used to endure.

Young, old and different ethnic races, they used to ask questions like did I use to wear braces?

I used to sit and think, am I a freak show? Subconsciously I started mumbling my words and keeping my voice nice and low. I thought that was the solution to make my problem go.

I became withdrawn in a social setting, why did I come? I was slyly regretting, spent periods of the evening worrying and fretting.

Little did I know, this was all within me, my brain was the lock and my tongue was the key. I started working on them simultaneously.

Building and developing a whole new me, if I can do it so can you, get in contact and we will help each other through, believe in yourself and whatever you decide to do but don't let your voice or situation determine you.

WRITTEN BY
MR LISP

(This poem/spoken word was written to give an insight into my life experiences and encounters battling with a speech impediment 'lisp', which I learned to overcome with self-confidence, awareness, and acceptance. If I can achieve it anyone can and will, you just have to believe and have focus and determination.)

"DON'T DIM
YOUR
LIGHTS,BECAUSE
OTHERS THINK
YOU SHINE
TO BRIGHT "
MR LISP 2022

A deeper insight into the man known as Mr Lisp, the name actually came about roughly 2 years ago during the first lockdown, I didn't choose the name, the name chose me, it fitted perfectly I have become a person that has no problem speaking my mind, so I thought the best thing is to address the elephant in the room by calling myself, Mr Lisp.

I am not sure what happened. I gather the additional time, lack of routine, and opportunity to really assess myself and life, I found my voice. I can't pinpoint a day, time, or place it just happened. I woke up one morning and said to my partner I'm going to embrace my voice and I'm going to take my spoken word/ poetry to new levels and heights.

So I started writing and entering competitions and open calls and I got my first bite which was from Kensington and Chelsea Art week (KCAW 2020) eternally grateful for the opportunity given.

And I would like to send a special thank you to Elisha Carter *(who is such a beautiful soul)* at The Cherrymoon 253 King's Rd, London SW3 5EL @thecherrymoonlondon where my work was displayed.

**KENSINGTON
+ CHELSEA
ART
WEEK**

**1-11 OCTOBER
2020**

POETRY CORNER

THE ROYAL BOROUGH

by Mr Lisp

Two borough's become one, that must be a recipe for order and fun.
The royal borough of Kensington and Chelsea, the smallest borough in
London, which host some of the biggest events to name a few.
The Chelsea Flower show, Notting hill Carnival, Kensington and Chelsea
Art week. It's a bustling, vibrant borough at its peak.
Arts, history and many hidden gems, great opportunity to explore, discover
and make new friends.
Express yourself, be who you want to be, art is self healing and bridges a
bond between you and me.
Art can tell a story, art can set a scene " The royal borough, was home to
the Queen"
Art is an expression I have to set free, Art allows me to discover my true
identity.
Trapped in the big wide world, in a rat race, art is my go to........ to slow
down the pace.
Art speaks a language of its own, an allows the individual to go into a
zone...... mind, body and soul, delve in deep, create and achieve, new and
existing goals.
We all have a purpose, believe and trust, creative self expression....... is
definitely a must.

This poem was selected as part of the KCAW20 Poetry Open Call in celebration of National Poetry Day

KCAW.CO.UK
@KCAWLONDON
#KCAW20

*(This was my first poem that I shared publicly "What an
amazing life-changing experience" truly humbling this
opportunity gave me focus, determination, and a massive
confidence boost, which really helped the transition to start
pursuing and sharing my work.)*

Let me backtrack, I've always been writing but I would never perform or really allow others to get lost in my work, and the handful of people who I did trust, use to encourage me to do more but I lacked self-confidence.

So I would like to take this opportunity to thank each and every one of you (*you know who you are*) as I wouldn't be the man that I am now if it wasn't for you guys believing in me, more than I believed in myself.

Thank You

MY JOURNEY

A couple of years ago, I decided to turn my life around.

How could I let my lisp keep me down?

How can I be fearing my own unique sound? Little did I know that's the diamond to my crown.

Outside Fairview house, with my sister and my wife, talking about the future, projects, and life.

My sister said to me I'm a chosen one and God has told me I need to use my voice and tongue, back then I said "sis that's not me", I will write behind the scenes for a ghost writer's fee.

Little did I know she had planted a seed and if you ask my wife she will totally agree.

A few months in, during the lockdown, I found the urge to release my sound, I entered competitions and started putting out work, the reaction, the love, and comments were berserk.

That gave me the incentive to strive and prevail and I learned I'm always going to be a winner even when I believe that I failed.

WRITTEN BY
MR LISP

(This particular piece was inspired by my sister and partner who was outside our old block discussing future plans and projects and without knowing they had planted the seed for me to start my journey.)

"THERE
IS ONLY
ONE YOU"
MR LISP
2022

This book means a lot to me more than I actually know and I hope I can inspire others to achieve their goals, dreams, and aspirations, like how I've been inspired.

I feel it's my duty and calling to share my thoughts, techniques, and inspiration to encourage and promote development, self-confidence, growth and inject positivity to all.

I have put pain, sweat, and tears into this book and what I have learnt throughout this journey and in life, what you sow is what you reap.

I was an individual who didn't fully believe in myself, I knew I had ability but didn't understand and fully believe in it, I was on a Rolla-coaster going around and around and had no idea how to get off. I was stuck in the rat race chasing a dream that I didn't know or believe in 100%.

One of the first things I learnt is you have to believe you're the best and obstacles are just another test that will always develop you, even if you can't see how at the present time, there is no such thing as failing, you have to take what you may believe is a failure as a lesson or a development opportunity, and you have to learn to adapt, self-evaluate and prepare for your next event, attempt or challenge no time to dwell or wallow in self-pity or doubt .

My main issue was self-confidence due to the fact I have a lisp, I decided to make my lisp dictate to me who I am, and what I can do (I take full accountability for my choices and poor decisions).

Accountability is the first hurdle I had to overcome "I had to admit that my lack of self-confidence allowed me to make poor choices, I subconsciously started to listen to when people were talking and the penny dropped (**RECOGNITION**) each and every one of us is unique and the voice is a distinctive trait that many of us possess.

I realized what I once believed was my obstacle, then became my shovel to help me on my path. I decided to embrace my lisp and now I'm no longer living in the shadow of my lisp or voice.

If I was to say it was plain sailing all the way I would be lying, it's been hard work, ongoing, and emotional at times and you really do get to learn about yourself inside out and outside in, so there is no escaping who you really are. You learn that you have to water your own garden first before you are able to water others, in other words, "I mean you have to look after yourself before you can effectively look after someone else."

The Cycle of change is something we all encounter when going through life changes and in general throughout life as we navigate through.

In theory the cycle of change is rather easy and straightforward, but in principle can be very difficult and can take a number of attempts, determination, and a real desire to change. I will explain the process in a very basic form, the cycle is broken down into six main sections

Pre-contemplation stage- Pre-contemplation is the unconscious stage where you are unaware or have no intention of changing your behaviour or working on a goal.

Contemplation stage- The contemplation stage is when you are aware a problem exists or you desire a change but there is no commitment to action changes.

Preparation stage- The preparation stage is where you have identified your goal and you have an intent on taking action to address the problem or goal.

Action stage- The Action stage is where you are implementing the new strategies, lifestyle, and behaviour techniques to gain your goal and objectives.

Maintenance stage- The maintenance stage is where you sustain your strategies, and your change of behaviour's and aim to replace the old ones to overcome existing issues or achieve desired goals if maintained you can exit the cycle.

Relapse stage- The relapse stage is where you revert back to old patterns of behaviour, at this stage, it is very important not to give up and self-evaluate to identify where you require more support, discipline, and structure then empower yourself to recontinue around the cycle to eventually obtain the exit.

Personally, I believe most people relapse due to the fact that they are not making changes because they want to and the change that they want is not coming from an organic place, they are either making changes to please others, fit in or are forced for other reasons i.e. health reasons, family commitments, etc. (*This also shows that regardless of the need to change, the desire and willingness needs to come from within.*)

As Individuals, we can get complacent and feel that we don't need to apply ourselves as much as before and in theory, we should be applying ourselves more to maintain our achievements and objectives as it is very easy to revert to old habits, some of these habits have been installed in us from a very young age and we are creatures of comfort so it is very easy to revert to what feels safe even though it can potentially be dangerous.

THE CYCLE OF CHANGE

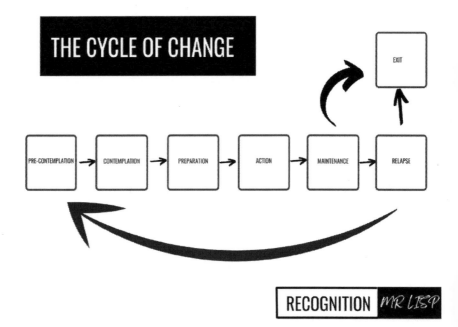

THE CYCLE OF CHANGE

PRE-CONTEMPLATION → CONTEMPLATION → PREPARATION → ACTION → MAINTENANCE → RELAPSE

EXIT

RECOGNITION MR LISP

THE CYCLE OF CHANGE

*We **PRE-CONTEMPLATE** without even knowing.*

*Throughout life, we continue to be growing. We get to a point where we need to make change, **CONTEMPLATE** and decide what's life choices and what is fate?*

*Knowledge, skill, and careful **PREPARATION** will propel you and guide you to your next destination.*

*It's time to take **ACTION**, you are in control implement the changes required to reach your goal, don't get complacent you have to **MAINTAIN** your flow, and this is key to maintain that you grow.*

*For some, this is the end of the cycle, but a cycle is like a revolving door a **RELAPSE** can bring your feet back to the floor, back to old behaviours, back to old routines, but if change is imminent, you've got to change the scene.*

You paint the picture, you tell the tale, you fill in the blanks with all the details, your hunger and determination will enable you to prevail.

WRITTEN BY
MR LISP

(This piece was written to explain the cycle of change, how fundamental it is for us to go through certain processes, and to identify why and how to make and sustain positive outcomes.)

Question if you were to look in the mirror and be honest with yourself, are you happy with what you see? (Not only referring to physical appearance) Are you being the true you? Are you happy in your relationship or are you just accepting what it is? Are you battling with identity? Are you happy with your career?

One of the first fundamental steps is growth and self-development it's about accepting who you are, this is what makes you unique, don't be afraid to be the square peg in a round hole.

Do not be who people tell you to be, be who you want to be. Throughout life, people are very good at dictating who they think you are or who you should be.

Each and every one of us, have our own unique heartbeat, fingerprint, DNA, and thought process, throughout life, it's very easy to adapt or change to fit into what we believe is the norm or socially acceptable. We all have our own story, tale or path that has got us to this point in life and it's about embracing your journey and also understanding that your journey doesn't define who you are, and who you will be.

UNIQUE

When I think of the word unique, it correlates beauty at its peak. The skin promotes beauty that runs so deep, the largest organ of over 20 square feet, it protects something so deep within ...something deeper than the scarification or the colour of your skin.

Each body has a story to tell, every bump, every bruise, every time that you win or lose, has been engulfed within creating a parallel dimension to another realm.

Expression!!!

This is your time to be free, use your story & your body as a lock and key, let me just say I'm not talking for a fee or sexually, I'm talking about visualizing..... heart, body, and soul... express, connect, achieve higher goals.

Close your eyes and set yourself free, you are perfect, entrust in the person you really want to be,

just allow me to go a little deeper, the darker the berry everything sweeter, higher vibrations, telepathic communication, emancipation, world liberation, all lives matter but blacks are the most targeted and misinterpreted nation.

Food for thought I'm going to leave that with you, a change of perspective, a whole different view.

WRITTEN BY
MR LISP

(This piece was written and based on a reflection of myself every scar, bruise, blemish, stretch mark, my lisp I had to learn to embrace and I want you to accept your uniqueness as it's you, it's yours, own it, don't be afraid to talk about it, be one with your inner being, that's the only way you will encounter true acceptance/freedom.)

(Personal Challenge-Look in the mirror and reflect on yourself, identify your uniqueness, embrace what you may believe are your flaws, and try to understand who you are, and why you are the way you are?)

BELIEVE IN YOURSELF

When you have a mission and a dream to fulfil, you don't have time to be idle, and still, you have to keep knocking at different, different doors, re-evaluate yourself and work on your flaws.

Be humble and willing to learn, cut yourself some slack, but still be firm, all work without no play, will turn you miserable, old, and possibly grey.

My favourite phrase is "what you sow is what you reap" and this is the prayer I say before I go to sleep "Now I lay me down to sleep; I pray the Lord, my soul to keep if I die before I wake, I pray the Lord my soul to take".

When you believe in yourself, you're destined to excel and you're still a winner even if you believe you fail.

God loves a trier and that's what I am, to work on your future you have to have a plan, you can't rely on chance to enable yourself to prevail and enhance.

We are living in a world that is callous and cold, where the rich get richer and the poor die overworked and cold.

working all the hours under the sun, but in the winter it's either heating or eating you decide which one?

We're living in a world that's really not fair, and it definitely has more than one tier, but save your breath because nobody cares.

WRITTEN BY
MR LISP

(This piece was inspired by my parents, as these were some of the positive affirmations, I grew up hearing and not really understanding the importance of them and implementing them accordingly too much later in life. I hope by sharing these with you they can have the same positive impact on you as they have had on me throughout life.)

" KEEP REACHING FOR THE STARS AND NEVER STOP UNTIL YOU GET THERE "
JEMZBYMARIE 2022

We all have all things that we believe are essential to us in life, and many times who and what we declare as essentials are materialistic or idolised. How many times have you heard "I can't live without my phone" or "Coffee is essential to my morning routine"?

Many of us dismiss our own personal needs, development, happiness, and health as they are not always tangible but are fundamental essentials.

THE ESSENTIAL FIVE

Essentials! essentials! essentials are things we can't live without, a mobile phone for a selfie and a pout.
When you think of essentials a few things come to mind, wi-fi, mobiles, bank cards, keys, and wine.
This is not an intensive list, just a mere few.
What is essential to me, may not be essential to you, as we are all unique individuals with different requirements and needs, we have a few essential things in common we all need to eat, drink, sleep, breathe and excrete.
These are the basics we need to survive, so I call them the essential five.
Essential workers kept the world ticking by and these are the heroes that nursed many cries.
It's essential to feel one with yourself, it's essential that you keep in optimum health.
It's essential to understand your requirements and needs, it's essential to nurture and protect the new batch of seeds.

Essentials are more than just me and you, essentials are things like paper for the loo, milk for your tea, contact lenses, and glasses to see.
So remember what is essential for you, may not be essential for me.

WRITTEN BY
MR LISP

(What is essential to you? This piece was written to provoke your thought process and highlight that we all have what we believe are our essential items and we tend to disregard the essential five and that our own development or self-love is essential.)

"MATERIALISTIC THINGS DIMINISH IN TIME, SO BE CAREFUL WHAT YOU FEED YOUR MIND" MR LISP 2022

Self-love is about understanding the balance between accepting yourself as you are but fully aware that you deserve better and you are willing to work towards achieving what you deserve.

Self-love can be split into a number of components but the main two are growth/development and mindset

Self-love is about loving yourself regardless, being tall, short, thick, or thin, you have to love the person inside to the core for example if you lose weight and your physical appearance changes that will not make you love yourself more it may boost your confidence but you are still the same person within thick or thin.

Your preference in individuals will change when you learn to love yourself. If you look back at when you were younger or in a different place than you are now, your preference in people, friends, or relationships has differed.

When you grow, develop and really identify with self-love, you tend to find that who and what you were attracted to prior, is not the same as now as you realise your worth, and what you will accept and what you will not.

What was once an attractive trait can now be perceived as childish, possessive, and possibly a lack of self-esteem?

When you truly love yourself, you release an aura that gives you a glow, which enables you to walk with your shoulders back and your head held high.

A confident person is highly attractive and stands out among the crowd.

Self-Love is commonly referred to or mistaken for selfishness and sometimes we have to be selfish to develop and grow, you have to become self-centred to truly develop and enable growth and be in a position to actively help and inspire others.

Your Mindset is fundamental, you have to make time for yourself, and realise that sleep, food, and general health are important to you, as well as believing in yourself and your ability.

Our minds are like sponges and we have to be fully aware of what we are allowing into our minds, so let us stop dwelling on negativity, plaguing ourselves with our inner thoughts of criticism, fear, and doubt, believing we are not enough, and constantly comparing ourselves to others.

" YOU CAN'T WATER SOMEONE ELSE'S GARDEN, IF YOUR WELL IS DRY" MR LISP 2022

SELF-LOVE

Self-Love is more than buying out the store. It's giving yourself the opportunity to open new doors.

Self-Love starts deep within, from the ointments and creams we apply to our skin, from the food we endure, to the company we keep, the number of hours of quality sleep.

Self-Love is about accepting who you are, and believing in your inner being!! That glistening star.

You're able to work on you, not for the acceptance of others and their vivid views.

Self-Love when accepted is beautiful, I just wish it was taught throughout school.

I love myself and I care about my health and collectively it can enhance my wealth.

I can't water your garden if my well is dry, so I change my mindset to "I will" or" I can try"

Once I am ok, then I can help you, then we can walk the path in unison, like a left and right shoe

WRITTEN BY
MR LISP

(This piece is written to identify what is self-love and how we neglect ourselves on a regular basis to please others or avoid dealing with a situation, problem or issue and if we don't accept, find a solution and process these we are unable to truly love ourselves, others and encounter true self-love, which is a feeling like no other.)

Self-love and your mindset will lead to the manifesting of positive and negative thoughts and the power of laws of attraction, this is a topic that many debate about and will continue to well after our time.

In my personal opinion I am a believer in the laws that govern the universe, in basic terms the law of attraction is the capabilities to attract into our lives whatever we are focusing on.

If you focus and dwell on negative thoughts you will remain in that circle of doom, sadness, and darkness you will remain under that dark cloud. If you focus on positive thoughts and have goals and dreams that you aim to achieve you will find a way to achieve them and see opportunities to assist you.

" IF YOU CAN DREAM IT, YOU CAN ACHIEVE IT"

MR LISP 2022

POSITIVITY

A positive vibe is engulfed from inside, a pure heart is an ideal start, positivity can be divided into two parts.

A physical presence with a unique essence, a mental state that determines your fate.

Believe in yourself, you're more than great, confidence is beautiful in every single way, so embrace yourself and enjoy every day.

Strive to achieve, believe to succeed, determination is the key to conceive, that's a play on words like the birds and the bees.

The key to success is not about being the best, it's about believing in yourself and withstanding life's test.

When you have that vibe, you're on a natural high, giving you the ability to walk with your head held high, your confidence beams, your aura infuses like steam. At this present moment you could be king or queen.

You are the best of the best, like Superman put a S on your chest, your positive energy could instantly kill any rodent or pest, not allowing the opportunity for negativity to manifest and hinder your vision, shape your decision, overall, not allowing you to complete your mission.

Remain, humble and focused, and stick to your goal, and your positive vibe will continue to flow.

WRITTEN BY
MR LISP

(This piece was written to encourage you to embrace positivity and the benefits. Positivity is beautiful, it is such a wonderful feeling. Positivity gives you an optimistic outlook on life, have you realised when we are positive, we engage in positive thinking, have positive emotions, and tend to engage in more positive behaviour.)

NEGATIVITY

A negative vibe begins inside, are you not adequate to be alive?

You could achieve but you don't believe, your positive vibe has been stolen by thieves, you feel suppressed, you are labelled as depressed.

You're thinking to yourself, you're not like the rest, but stop comparing, it is not a contest.

Good things can't happen to me, I have lost my key of opportunity.

Why am I dumb, thick, and pessimistic? and I can never change as they say "mud sticks."

I walk around with a deep dark cloud, I am miserable, down with a permanent frown.

I should be an individual and change the mould, I should live my life with purpose, not callous and cold.

I should be the s#*t and not the blue bottle fly, don't say I can't, I should always say I'll try.

I should give my all and be the best of the best, but I can't because my life's a mess. I'm suffering from anxiety and self-induced stress, and every time I look in the mirror, I love myself less.

(This piece was written to express how negativity can plague you throughout all aspects of your life, if allowed to manifest and consume you, with a pessimistic mindset you find problems in every situation, which carries you deeper into the black hole.)

I am a firm believer that happiness is paramount and only you can truly make yourself happy. Why do something that doesn't make you happy? And this can be related to all aspects of your life from personal choices, relationships, friendships, careers, dreams, and goals.

You have the choice and overall control to shape any decision that you encounter. It is for you to identify, what the choices are and what is important to you *(and they will change)* and how much you want to pursue your happiness.

Sometimes to obtain happiness the path and journey will not be smooth, and you will be tempted to quit or choose an easier less rewarding route, but you have to remember difficulties and hurdles develop and grow you throughout.

"They say pressure makes diamonds" so when you reach your objective you can and will "shine bright like a diamond" remember what comes easy, generally tends to go easy and if it was easy to obtain or didn't require commitment, focus, dedication, and boundaries then everyone would or will be doing it.

Life is short and to me, it is about living and enjoying it to the max, do what makes you truly happy as happiness is paramount, only you know what makes you happy and what self-fulfillment you require to obtain your needs to achieve your over happiness, just like love, happiness is an emotion which can also have a positive and negative impact on your life choices.

HAPPINESS

Only you can truly make yourself happy, so be true to yourself and understand who you are. Look up to the sky you can relate to that star, you easily outshine every star by far.

Happiness is an emotional state, a feeling that feels super great, you smile and you don't know why? You can be so overwhelmed, to the point you cry and those tears I call tears of joy, just like when the midwife says it's a girl or a boy.

True happiness is about embracing yourself, being comfortable within, content, and happy with every inch of your skin.

Harmony and peace flows throughout, as during negative times happiness was on a drought

Happiness can give you a purpose more than you know, it's like an iceberg only a tip is on show, so dig deep and don't be afraid to jump in with both feet, because when the opportunity of happiness comes you don't want to be caught asleep.

The opportunity to be happy can arise each and every day. It's for you to identify, encase it and try to make it stay.

WRITTEN BY
MR LISP

(What is happiness to you? This piece was written to get you thinking about happiness and what happiness is and means to you, it is important to remember that happiness is different for everyone so like many things in life there is no wrong or right as we are all unique individuals.)

We all have goals, dreams, and ambitions not many individuals achieve or try to obtain them, as many don't know where to start, don't believe in themselves and their abilities, or have allowed others to kill or suppress their dreams, maybe you have tried before and failed and now given up.

Goals, dreams, and aspirations are beautiful and sometimes the sole reason why we continue on our paths

We constantly hear the word goals used throughout life but what is a goal? Your Goal can be anything you have a desire to achieve, something you plan and commit to obtaining.

Your dreams are something you have visioned, which can be converted into a goal. Your aspirations are your dreams, ambitions, and hopes in achieving your desired goals

Setting goals for yourself is imperative. It gives you a sense of direction and purpose in life, having the ability to sit, reflect and think about what you want out of life. Setting goals can put the ownership back on yourself to get a grasp on your life by acknowledging what you desire out of life.

Setting goals can give you the motivation required to achieve them, setting goals can also help you see the grand picture, it enables you to prioritise what is important within your life.

If you look at it like this, a dream recorded in whatever format i.e. written down with a date becomes a goal, a goal segmented into steps becomes a plan and your plan supported by your actions makes your dreams come true.

When setting goals, it is effective to use the SMART technique, this particular method gives you the ability to make specific goals and measure your progress.

SMART is an acronym used to describe the technique of setting goals. The acronym stands for **SPECIFIC, MEASURABLE, ATTAINABLE, REALISTIC,** and **TIME-BOUND**.

S for specific. A goal should be specific, precise, and clear which can make them easier to achieve.

M for measurable. A goal should be measurable which you can track, measure progress and identify if the goal has been obtained.

A for attainable. Goals should be clear, challenging but attainable.

R for realistic. Is your goal realistic in this lifetime

T for time bound. We have to have a deadline to keep us motivated.

" SET A GOAL,
THAT WILL
KEEP YOU ON
YOUR TOES "
MR LISP 2022

GOALS, DREAMS, AND ASPIRATIONS

The SMART technique is the greatest way, you get to use your head and a technique that you can use day to day.

We all have goals and dreams, and for so many, they got diminished in their teens, you can never be too old to set a new goal, climb Mount Everest with a flag and pole.

Anything can be accomplished, obtained, and ceased, but you have to work hard beyond what the eyes can see.

You have to have discipline, boundaries, and rules and it's down to you to install the appropriate tools.

Find your why, because that why will change your" I can't" to "I can" and "I will try"

Pursue your dreams, give yourself a purpose and a goal and don't be afraid to take back the passion that FEAR has stole.

WRITTEN BY
MR LISP

(This piece was written as an affirmation to help myself and hopefully you to stay focused, motivated and ready to identify your goals, dreams, and aspirations. I would like to highlight that new goals, dreams and aspirations can be set

at any time or age, you're never too old, you just have to be willing to work on them.)

Even when you feel like you've reached your goal, set another, keep aspiring daily, each and every day that you wake up, you have been blessed with another opportunity, so seize it and make it happen "carpe diem" as life is short and we don't have forever.

Please scan the QR code below for a template of the DREAMS AND GOALS SMART TECHNIQUE plus other templates. Please feel free to use or amend to your peril.

SCAN QR FOR FREE EXAMPLE TEMPLATES

Sometimes it's good to feel uncomfortable as that means growth, development, or valuable lessons will be learned, if you are comfortable, you tend not to push yourself beyond what you believe is capable, you don't aspire to want more or do more.

Life is about giving your best, those who work harder, study harder, and train harder are generally more successful in achieving their goals.

It's the little details that count the extra hour, pushing yourself that little bit further, the extra reps, as with repetition and consistency it can amount to a major difference over a period of time.

Take a moment, a day, a week, however long that you believe is required to think about what you want and where you want to be, or what you want to achieve?

We have to have dreams or goals in life or we become stagnant or mediocre (basically humans that just exist) and you have to decide what type of person you want to be.

The individual that strives to excel constantly trying to supersede their circumstances or do you want to be an individual that just exists, afraid to try anything new or somewhat challenging?

Some people are comfortable with mediocrity, but are you? They allow hard work or challenge to prevent them from living a better or greater life.

To live a better life, you need to find your inner greatness.

Greatness is within you, greatness is becoming the greatest version of yourself and demolishing the boundaries or restrictions that we allow to hold us captive in a place, situation or life to the point we just settle.

Let me put this out there, there is nothing wrong with being either, but you have to make that choice and I am afraid only you can do it, you may find other factors such as family, friends, lifestyles, etc, can have an impact, but overall, it's your decision and it doesn't mean you are tied to your decision as throughout life things change.

EXCEL OR EXISTED

Do you want to excel or exist?

To EXCEL you have to be willing to fail, learn from your mistakes, and push through even when it starts to ache, as determination is the key to success, boundaries and self-confidence will bring out the best, they say sleep is the cousin of death, so that's 365 days with minimal rest.

Each day is a new opportunity and there's more to this world than your eyes can see and you have to play the game like it is Monopoly, no chance, no community chest, you just have to be wise and allocate where you invest.

To EXIST you don't need structure, a plan, or a to-do list, you just get on by, spending hours on social media sharing, retweeting, and saying hi, afraid to step out of your comfort zone, anything too challenging, you're giving up and going home.

Let me stick to what I know, afraid of change and scared to grow, not happy with your job but it pays the bills, but you don't have the courage to go and make your deal, no get up and go, no additional drive, happy to spend your weekend watching Facebook live, admiring your friends, wishing you could be like them.

The choice is yours, decide who you want to be, there's no wrong or right so your choice is free.

WRITTEN BY
MR LISP

(This piece was written to get you thinking about who you are? Are you happy or just content? Who do you want to be? Life is constantly about making decisions and choices but overall, the choice is always going to be yours.)

" LIFE IS ABOUT CHOICES"
MR LISP 2022

The person you want to be is based on you, the tv programmes you watch, the books you read, and the people you socialise with they all will and can have an impact on your life and throughout your transitioning journey you will soon identify who, what, when, where and how these, fall into place within your chosen path and trust me somethings, people, etc, will be left behind.

You have to learn to understand and accept that everything runs its course from friendships, relationships, careers, and even life. So don't be afraid to outgrow your situation, social and support networks, it is perfectly normal

This can be hard to understand for example "You are usually the social one, the party starter, centre of attention, the limelight person. To what may appear all of a sudden to you, you discover you are no longer in the mood or have the desire to attend all the events, and you are opting out and preferring to staying in at home."

You may start to find that you and your peers don't seem to have as much in common as before and that you are on different pages in life, where they may be comfortable, you are not and you need and require more (and this is totally normal).

Once you identify this (and it may be brought to your attention by others) I call this the transitioning stage and it can happen with what appears to be out of the blue, but actually, it has been an ongoing process, like a seed that has been planted the roots have been growing behind the scene but your unable to visually see your flower or plant until it germinates through the soil.

This particular period can be absolutely beautiful as your starting to look at life and yourself from a different point of view, you will start to learn about yourself in more depth, what ignites your fire, your personality and thought process may alter, and your morals, standards, and confidence may also enhance or alter plus many more identifiable traits.

Challenge-Feel free to sit down, reflect and identify and note down any changes you have encountered thus far.

"DON'T BE AFRAID
TO THINK OUTSIDE
OF THE BOX "
MR LISP 2022

COMPETE

When you supersede the intellectual, equilibrium of your peers, you start to deliberate with voices between your ears, you realize that the battle comes from within, so swallow that pride and thicken that skin.

Twisted fate is my destiny and the only two individuals that can alter that is God and me.

The past is what shapes us! The present is now! The future is uncertain and can't be detailed.

In life we were born to compete, think of the millions of feet that pound our streets. Each individual is a potential threat, divide, conquer and challenge what's next.

Compete against yourself to be the best of the best, and challenge yourself daily, till you are laid to rest.

Wake up in the morning believing to be a winner, think like a caveman, and bring home the dinner.

WRITTEN BY
MR LISP

(This piece was written in reflection of my own transitioning experience where I found myself wanting and needing more deeper, meaningful, and powerful thought-provoking conversations with my peers which I was unable to obtain and could not understand why.)

As much as the transitioning process can be amazing it can also be very confusing and very challenging as you can encounter battles with trying to fit in amongst your peers which can result in you conforming to be socially accepted. This is a common trait and can leave you highly confused as at one point this is all you knew, this was your foundation, but it is no longer who you are and what you are about.

At this point is where your personal challenge begins and you start to understand who is a Crab or an Ant.

When I talk about Crabs and Ants, I am referring to the metaphor of crab mentality also known as crabs in a bucket. Which I will briefly explain in my own words.

"If you were to place crabs in a bucket, instead of working collectively together to escape, they will prevent one another from excelling and escaping their current circumstances with the thought process "If I can't escape, neither can you" so we will all remain in this bucket pinching one another if any tries to escape, each crab is thinking about oneself.

In comparison to the ants, one of the smallest insects in the world, they know about determination, strength, and collaborative teamwork. Have you seen an ant carrying food or other resources i.e. a leaf? You will see a number of ants working together collectively to carry the item and achieve the desired outcome all for one and one for all.

Throughout your life, you will find yourself surrounded by crabs and ants and it is for you to identify who is who (but they will also identify themselves at some point.)

These can be long-term friends, your significant other, or even family members (so don't be surprised). Embrace the identifying challenge and stay true to yourself and you will excel in all aspects.

CRABS AND THE ANTS

As I reflected on my family, friends, and peers, the people that have been around me for numerous years. I have to say this with a heavy heart many got dropped as I made my new start, one of the hardest things I've had to do, but sacrifices happen when you have dreams to pursue.

Not many understood my journey, they would tease me if I went to bed early, and conversation just were not the same. I needed something that would intellectually stimulate my brain and I was fed up of hearing about cars and chains, Brazilian weave, and who's next to conceive.

I wanted a conversation that was mind-blowing and deep, topics that I researched before I went to sleep.

Who was going to support me, who was going to hold me back, who would try to knock me off focus, who would try to keep me on track?

I had to persevere, I would upload work but hardly anyone would share. If there was a party or function, I can guarantee everyone would be there, uploading videos with no care or hesitation to share.

A handful of people is now how the circle remains, you know who you are, no need to mention names.

As the saying goes show me who your friends are and I will tell you who you are.

I guess my friends are astronomical objects, because I am a certified star.

WRITTEN BY
MR LISP

(Can you relate to Crabs and the Ants? *This piece summarises a true-to-life account of what I was going through and the battles I was enduring to pursue my dreams throughout my life. You will be in similar situations, persevere in a forward direction to obtain your goals.*)

Time is of the essence, understanding time and what can be achieved if goals, self-reflection, evaluation, discipline, boundaries, and organisational skills are put in place.

I hear numerous people (myself included at one point) say "There are just not enough hours in a day" or "If I had more time I could or would have done this or that".

In reality, 24 hours (1440 minutes or 86,400 seconds) in a day is more than enough time if you are disciplined, focused, and working towards a structure and goal.

The number of seconds, minutes, and hours that are wasted *(not used to an individual's full capabilities per day, also known as unproductive time.)* Due to social media, lack of planning and organisational skills, lack of discipline and structure, focus and drive for example individuals who don't have a routine tend to go sleep late, wake up late, poorer diet due to nocturnal lifestyles, and generally are more chaotic individuals, without discipline and structure.

Disclaimer not all individuals this is just a mere observation over the years

WASTED TIME

As I put pen to paper I'm inspired by my creator, giving me the ability to strive for much greater, time is one of the only things you can't get back, that's not an opinion that's actually a fact.

If you believe in the higher power, you do not want to waste a second in a minute, enclosed in an hour, trapped in a day, which is embraced in a week, which is correlated in a month, which is times by 12....... which is totaling a year. So if you waste a second you can see how it can affect your year.

How many hours do we spend online? Is wasted time really a crime? Why do we all justify with the same significant line?" I am only on there to pass the time."

We have all been given a number and our lives on the clock and the only guarantee that we hold is that it will stop, no more beating, no tick tock, be a shepherd and herd the sheep, instead of being a sheep and follower of the flock.

Be your own person and believe in yourself, because your own unique beat is what keeps you on your feet, have a plan that you partly understand.

Work to your goals, and don't let anybody knock you off your toes, some people walk with a deep dark soul, a black cloud that darkens your light, but you got to dig deep and fight with all of your might and don't stop until you reach and embark on that light, ask for help, don't be ashamed, go grab your purpose, rejoice and reclaim, believe in yourself as your more than just a name.

The process of time is such a beautiful thing, a rare commodity that can be seen between a child and an adult's skin

WRITTEN BY
MR LISP

(This piece was written when I was in a self-reflective mode, analysing my own use of time, how important time is, and realising that it shouldn't be wasted or taken for granted. I was able to identify that I was spending too much unproductive time.)

Time is something we all have, it's how we use our time, which impacts on our results. We all have 24 hours in a day and the question is how come others can complete all their daily tasks and manage to do extracurricular activities i.e. starting a business, pursuing new ventures, extra time with family. The secret is these individuals have structure, routine, boundaries, a plan to execute their goals and dreams, and the determination to succeed at whatever cost.

I challenge you to implement a realistic routine which you have to adhere to try to give it your all (110%) as you will only be benefitting yourself and your significant others, you need to have discipline and be willing to push yourself beyond your normal expectation. If done correctly it will not be easy and will push you beyond your expectations and definitely will make you a more organised individual, disciplined, and aware of productive time and non-productive time and how impactful it can be if allocated accordingly.

Aim to do 30 days *(as they say it takes 30 days to develop a habit)*

Please scan the QR Code below for an example template this is just a reference feel free to use and expand to your needs and requirements or use a particular method that you will believe will work for you.

SCAN QR FOR FREE EXAMPLE TEMPLATES

When implementing your time management plan, aim to be realistic, segment your day realistically and accordingly, and set goals and targets that will push you, but are not unobtainable which can result in you giving up and believing you have failed.

If your unable to stick to your plan don't beat yourself up about it, sit down and self-evaluate (or get in contact and we can address the situation and try to implement a new method that can be implemented) and try to identify why you are unable to complete or adhere to your plan.

When you are able to identify the factors that are holding you back i.e. distractions, social media, family, not believing in yourself, unable to break pre-existing life cycles, you will be able to implement additional changes to help you succeed.

For a change there has to be a desire, willingness to sacrifice, and the drive to achieve, and with that comes boundaries if you do not put your goals, dreams and ambitions first no else will.

You have to be selfish *(at times)* focused, driven and be willing to put work in beyond other's expectations and even your own.

Remember your actions will equal your results and there is nothing you can't achieve if you put your mind to it.

BOUNDARIES AND RULES

Boundaries and rules are important tools and they can easily be misinterpreted by small-minded fools, not every rule is about containment, believe in yourself and make that statement.

You have to install boundaries to protect yourself, and I'm not only referring to your mental health, boundaries and rules can keep you on track and they can also be a barrier against an enemy's attack.

Structure and discipline are imperative and without them, it's pointless like trying to carry water in a sieve.

Due dates and deadlines unfortunately they have to be done, so you have to have a balance between work and fun.

You have to have order to know what is next, and you're not obligated to reply to that text, prioritize what needs to be done and tick off the list one by one.

WRITTEN BY
MR LISP

(Do you have boundaries and rules in place for yourself? This poem/spoken word was written as a summary and part of my daily affirmation which I used to keep myself motivated, focused and was an influential support tool to aid the boundaries and rules I had implemented for myself while

writing this book, a keynote is nothing is set in stone so boundaries and rules can and will alter.)

If you have a burning desire inside that you can't suppress, you have to tune into that feeling, emotion, dream, or goal as you will always feel incomplete, a sense of loss and dissatisfaction.

You generally find your passion not for what you do, it is for why you do it, and that "**WHY**" is your motivator, your heartbeat, the flickering flame, that knot in your stomach, that's your engine you have to take that **WHY** to pursue your goals and dreams.

Personally speaking, when you've found your **WHY** it becomes an issue in your life, you eat, sleep, and dream your goals and how you're going to achieve them, I found making a plan that I understood made my goals more attainable as they say "fail to plan, prepare to fail" discipline and structure are fundamental you have to have boundaries and a balance or you will get burnt out or can lose focus very easily.

Any spare time I had, became engulfed in achieving, I would find myself making notes, daydreaming constantly thinking about how I can excel and what is my next steps. It is such a powerful experience when passion, drive, positivity, and focus combine into a collective force that is hard to be broken.

Many times, as individuals we like things to be perfect, very textbook but life can be very, unpredictable so a solid bit of advice is "ride the wave "and what I mean by that is go with the flow if things get tough you get tougher and don't give up as there is always a calm after every storm and when things settle your vision can and will become clearer.

WHY

Why do you want to be successful?

Why do you want to achieve your goals?

What is driving you in life? What is keeping you on point like the tip of the knife?

Why does it hurt when you don't achieve?

Why do you get that feeling deep within, that same feeling that gives you goosebumps on your skin?

Why do you feel incomplete?

Why do you feel like you're bringing nothing to the table but you're occupying a seat?

Why do you want more?

Why do you feel like you're going through revolving doors?

So many whys, what's next in store only you can create your path and unlock your door.

WRITTEN BY
MR LISP

(This piece was written to get you thinking about your why and for you to self-reflect on yourself. We are plagued with why's from we are born just like our goals, our why's can and will change.)

Sometimes you have to sit down and have a heart-to-heart with yourself take a look at yourself deeply don't be afraid to open up some scars, and address any pre-existing issues to completely move forward and excel in life.

sometimes the only person you can reason *(talk)* with is yourself (*and this doesn't mean you have mental health issues*) it just means you get a deeper level insight into yourself, which only you can access, understand and change.

Life is about development and growth, and you find that from within, self-confidence is so beautiful, its presence can light up a room, it can make you stand out among others like a rose amongst thorns.

You have to have self-confidence as you're the only person who can truly push yourself to the limits, you're the only person who knows your journey the trials and tribulations, to your success, so you have to remain strong, focused, and have self-belief within yourself, don't be afraid of hard work as hard work will always prevail over talent that doesn't work hard.

Heart to Heart

I had to have a heart to heart and reason with myself to work out if I'm doing justice for myself and my health or if I'm obsessed with the fame and the wealth.

I had to dig deep, I even opened up some scars, now I feel like a wreck that's been hit by six cars.

I took that feeling from deep within, every time that I lost, every time I didn't win, every time I fornicated, swore, or sinned. I rolled it up and put it straight in the bin.

And I reinstalled my software win, win, win, now my brain has a new system of processing things.

I can do it, I can achieve, I will supersede any opportunity, my mind is courageous, my mind is great, when I came into this world, I was given a date, the time in between is where I need to concentrate because my expiry date is chosen by fate, not a minute early or a second late, so the middle part is where my legacy is made, so this is the point I've got to put the work in because when I am done, I'm going up with the kings.

WRITTEN BY
MR LISP

(This piece was inspired by a real sit-down heart-to-heart I had with myself I was at a point in my life where I challenged if what I was doing was correct, and I had to readdress some personal issues to be able to move on accordingly, sometimes the only person you can really get the truth from is yourself.)

Your emotions can take you on a whirlwind adventure and can easily put a spanner in the works, one moment you can be focused, and highly motivated, then next you are at a point where you are thinking and saying "what is the point, this is a waste of time." And this can be due to a number of reasons from happiness, joy, sadness, anger etc.

I personally went through this myself; I experienced a tsunami of emotions which I collectively put into the word grief.

I would describe grief as sorrow to an indescribable level, it is so intense it hurts beyond words, a feeling like no other that overcomes you.

I was feeling nothing but grief and heartbreak, I lost faith, friendships, family, and even myself. I no longer focused on my dreams, I never planned anything I was living day by day looking back it was a very chaotic time. I didn't know where to go and how to push myself to continue to thrive in life.

I lost my twins in December 2014 and I can honestly say I have never been the same, when I say emotions, I think I experienced them all within one moment. The joy of seeing your children being born, knowing that they are not going to survive, from joy to grief, anger, and pain, that instant feeling of going insane, that's when I disregarded faith I believed if God was real, he/she would have kept them safe, I blamed myself for many things. I can now openly talk about the situation as time is the greatest healer and trust me each day it does get slightly easier.

I am now in a better place, I have rekindled the love and joy that I have in faith. I found my focus and decided to take my pain and transfer it into whatever I do which became my why, my engine, and the fuel to my fire.

STILL NOT AFRAID TO SHED A TEAR

Let me have your ears for a minute or two, have you ever lost someone that's close to you?

I'm going to talk straight from the heart, no more introduction, just let me start,14th of the 12th 2014, I lost my prince and princess on the same day, had them in my arms as I felt their heartbeats fade away,

I felt a feeling that I've never felt before all I know was it hurt down to the core, that sensation is what I call pain, those neurotransmitters really affected my brain, and since then, my logical thinking has never been the same, holding them motionless I felt so numb, I looked to the left and I saw their mum lost, grief-stricken, heartbroken all in one, then the burden hit, how am I going to break this to my son.

I felt like my world was caving in, I reasoned with myself and said it's karma for my sins and I wish I went to church every Sunday, instead of raving, playing football, and making girls the main focus of my day.

My heart was broken, I'm surprised it still beat. I should have never skipped leg day at the gym, as all this weight is upon my feet and now they're giving in, wanting to cry but my tear ducts were dry.

Why didn't God take me? they were too young to die. Minutes on this earth I gather God decided they have already done their worth, and they should be returned to live in paradise, instead of this world that is so cold, prejudice, and far from nice.

My head, it was all over the place, and I still get flashbacks of the doctor's face, and medical negligence I definitely have a case.

Watching them getting weighed, tagged, and dressed, I had to hold them one more time close to my chest, I closed my eyes wishing it was all a dream, and when my eyes refocused, I was in the same scene.

When the minutes turned to hours, and hours turned to days, I barely ate and I never had a shave, hanging over my head I still had to put them in the grave. Days became weeks and weeks became months, pallbearers, flowers, and wreaths and I was feeling nothing but heartache and grief, ashes to ashes and dust to dust my twins are in God's hands one of the only people I totally trust,

Grief it's such a weird thing, it takes you to a place where you don't know where to begin. They say time is the greatest healer and that is so true so when the months become years, I'm not afraid to still shed tears.

WRITTEN BY
MR LISP

(This piece was inspired by a personal life-changing challenge that I had to overcome the hardest test in life I have had to deal with to date, this is a summary of the events and emotions. If anyone has gone through similar

situations or currently dealing with a challenging situation feel free to get in contact if you require any additional support or help to access additional services.)

Your emotions can also have a positive affect and change your outlook and may push you to pursue new ventures, goals, and dreams and this is generally caused due to happiness, love, and contentment within life. Love is an emotion that can play with our minds. It can propel you into the unexpected, it can have you waking up smiling, and feeling super motivated and wanting more out of life.

The feeling of love can make you feel happy, and generally, when an individual is happy their mindset changes and allows them to be more open-minded and able to fulfil goals, dreams, and ambitions. Each emotion can have a positive or negative impact on you as an individual, what you have to remember emotions change. So sometimes instead of fighting them ride the wave and steer it to your advantage.

"TO LOVE
AND TO
BE TRULY
LOVED
IS A
FEELING
LIKE NO
OTHER"
MR LISP
2022

Love

What is love?

The definition of love is unknown to man.

It's a feeling that only you can truly understand.

We all have our perception of what we believe, but true love can make you weak at the knees.

It can take your voice and leave you unable to speak. As you sow, so shall you reap.

It can manipulate you like it is a game, and it can get to your head like stardom and fame.

In severe occasions it can leave you insane, crying, sobbing, heartache, and pain.

Love is a four-letter word that is freely used, misinterpreted, battered, and often abused.

Think before you open your heart and be careful who you choose.

Love can reinstall your faith, and leave you feeling secure and safe.

Love can have you in such a happy place, and make a smile a permanent fixture on your face.

Love can re-energise your soul, giving you the strength to fulfil your goals

Love is a mix of deep emotions, no fairy godmothers, no spells or potions. Love is generated from within, it can't be contained in a bottle or a tin.

WRITTEN BY
MR LISP

(This piece is thought-provoking and each and every one of us can relate to aspects, if not all elements of this piece, Love is strange but wonderful at the same time, we all have the ability to give and receive love, and if we want more love, we need to give more love.)

WHAT DOES LOVE MEAN TO YOU?

_____

_____

_____

_____

_____

_____

_____

Within life we need to all sit, and reflect, how often do you sit and reflect? Reflection is a great way to analyse your life, self-evaluate and look back at possible choices and actions that have had a positive and negative impact on yourself and others and what you would do differently if you could or would.

This is a great learning tool to develop goals, accept accountability, and be able to make more proactive decisions in aid of good.

REFLECTION

As I look back on myself, I try to justify my life, have I made the right decisions, have I chosen the right wife?

Is this career for me? Should I have negotiated my fee? up until this point have I done my best? What would have happened if I had revised for my tests?

If I had implemented structure and boundaries, would my house have white picket fences and be surrounded by trees?

If I applied myself more, would I still be so poor? If I ate more greens, would I have the youth from my teens?

If I put an extra hour in each day, would it be reflected in my salary and my pay?

What I didn't know, I had control over my life and didn't have to deal with certain struggles and strife. I just had to be true to myself, and identify the importance of my health and my wealth.

I decided to put respect on my name, and since then nothing has been the same, people look at me differently, take me seriously, judge me on my ability, no longer on my skin tone or how I appear physically.

You have to make a stand, sometimes don't be afraid to march without a band, as you have to blow your own trumpet loud, so others can hear you and understand that your proud.

WRITTEN BY
MR LISP

(This piece was written to inspire you to reflect on yourself, think about your life, the choices you made, and whether they were the best. With hindsight what would you have done differently (if anything) and how are you going to move forward?)

"TO ACHIEVE
YOU HAVE TO
LOOK BEYOND
WHAT THE EYES
CAN SEE "
MR LISP 2022

Many times, throughout life we try to justify our actions by blaming, offloading, and projecting onto others for the misfortunes in our lives or the lack of discipline, boundaries, and rules we have installed we have to remember if something is important to us, we will find a way regardless, if it is not important, we will find an excuse. To be quite frank it can be easier to justify than take accountability but that's a self-development goal for many, to achieve and acknowledge accountability over justification.

JUSTIFY

These are some phrases I hear all the time, some can be bitter and sour like lime.

I have compiled them into a story once upon a time. I'm not saying the reasons couldn't be true, but I will leave you to decide to determine your view

Little Billy, was known to be silly, his mum Charlene was the justify queen, but life's been hard, she had Billy as a teen

From the age of three, he was addicted to Mc D's but Charlene would say "it's only a treat" this happened to be 7 days of the week,

When the Social worker Claire used to knock on the door, Billy would get angry and throw tantrums on the floor, Charlene would say "he's never done this before and maybe he's tired from the walk to the store."

Charlene was prone to getting calls from the school, Billy not listening he was being the class fool

"The reason why he doesn't pay attention is because he has ADHD"

Even though he's not diagnosed, that's what google told me."

"The reason that he's rude, I'm a woman, not a dude, I don't know how to be a man being a single parent wasn't in my plan"

"The reason he never passed, the teacher never liked him in the class". But Billy's school friends said he never completed his task.

Little Billy clocked on that he can't do wrong, and his mum would be there to defend him strong.

"The reason why he lost his job is because he was black", not because he was lazy and trying to slack.

"The reason he's in prison for a horrendous crime, he was with his friends, at the wrong place, wrong time."

Justify can be another word for an excuse, a get out of jail card, something to be used.

If you can sit and justify the actions in life, are you truly happy with your partner, husband, or wife? Decisions, decisions they make the time go by.... but in reality, many of us should really say goodbye. If we did there wouldn't be so many victims of domestic violence in the sky. RIP to everyone who has passed on by.

Can you justify who you really are? Is your life sparkling, just like a star?

Every action has a reaction and I believe in laws of attraction, so what I put out I'm going to get back, some call it karma, I call it facts.

WRITTEN BY
MR LISP

(Are you a Justify king or queen or do you know one? What is your opinion of Charlene? How many of these phrases have you heard? It is so easy to justify actions throughout our lives, as humans, we have a tendency to avoid, divert and project onto others, without taking accountability for our own actions, this piece was written to get you thinking/ reflecting about yourself and are you a justify king or queen. NB this is a fictional piece)

Life is about accountability we have to be able to hold our hands up and admit when we're wrong, don't be ashamed to say we don't know or understand, don't feel inferior stand up and voice your opinion, if you believe in something stand by it even if you're on your own be the shepherd, not the sheep.

Sometimes we need to take accountability for our own actions as deep within we all know "right from wrong" and that "every action has a reaction" and there are pros, cons, and consequences to every decision we make.

You own your thoughts and opinions, don't be afraid to voice and share, even if others don't want to hear or acknowledge you, stand by your opinions, and believe in yourself accountability will separate you from the average.

"DON'T BE AFRAID TO ADMIT YOUR WRONG"
MR LISP 2022

ACCOUNTABILITY

You have to show accountability throughout your life, stand by your choices even if others don't think it's right, believe in yourself your future is bright.

If you have something to say, say it with your chest, you don't think like the others, because you were never made like the rest.

Don't be afraid to apologise, say sorry and look them in the eyes. Accountability means you can admit when you are wrong, you get straight to the point no long-winded song.

You say what you do, you do what you say, being accountable is the only way, It will gain you respect, and you will live your life with fewer regrets, for progression and change accountability is the next step

We all know wrong from and right, so it's my decision if I flee or fight.

I have to stand by my decisions in the end, so it's my choice if we deport or remain friends.

WRITTEN BY
MR LISP

(Are you accountable for your actions? Do you stand by what you say? This piece was written to resonate with your inner being and awaken your accountable trait, sometimes we don't think about accountability as it's easier to justify we all do it, but to make positive forward progress within life we have to be accountable, it makes you, you. You are an

individual that can take ownership without pointing a finger even though it could have a negative consequence for you. Accountability puts you in a different league, you can gain honour and respect, and you're able to live your life with fewer regrets.)

Pressure makes diamonds, you have to prove to yourself why you deserve to achieve your goals as in life many will doubt you or wish for you to fail.

Don't forget to pat yourself on your back, as with development and hunger we tend not to acknowledge and celebrate our achievements and dwell on what has not been accomplished as of yet, with that being said you don't want to get complacent as it's easy to lose your focus, hunger, and sight of your target.

With personal development, you have to have a balance or you will either get burnt out or despise your goal or target, you have to have a personal life which in turn can give you the fuel to keep you going an allowing you to continue to chase your dreams, as they say, "work hard, play harder."

BALANCE

In life we have to have a balance between work and play, you can't work every hour, till you're old and grey.

Make time for your family, yourself, and friends make plans for the weekend as Monday you are back to the grind again!!

Focus!!! Get back on task, A1 student top of the class, employee of the week, top of the charts, late nights, and early starts.

If you work hard, you have to play hard, fun times, good food and jokes, herbal bubble bath, relax and soak.

Self-indulge, recreate your goals, mind over matter, detoxify the soul, and don't be afraid to have an early night and wake up early with your future Insight.

They say the early bird catches the best worm, so make sure your structure and routine are strict and firm.

WRITTEN BY
MR LISP

(Do you have balance in your life? This piece was written to highlight effective balance, work life, social life, personal time and pampering, growth, and personal development. Balancing your life is a skill and one of the hardest things to do especially as each day is different and your daily demands can change, you may not be obtaining a 50/50 balance in your life and personally, I don't think anyone is, but if your balance is more than 70/30 for a prolonged time, I would recommend you re-evaluating your life balance as

this will be taking a toll on some element of your life i.e. health, family, relationships, wealth and growth.)

Before you judge someone, try walking a day in their shoes and see if it's a path for you, as things can be very different from what we see, not everything that sparkles are diamonds and social media has really shown us this

Question. How many times have you gone on social media and looked at someone's pictures or videos and believe they are living their best life, they have hit the jackpot, their life's perfect and it can make you even question your own life. Why can't I go on endless holidays? How come I don't attend these types of events, why is my life so boring an uneventful?

The issue is over 85% of us only upload what we perceive to be conversation starters, self-gratification worthy, and ego-boosting, so basically, we show you, what we want and can portray our lives to be something it's not, sometimes we will never understand another person's journey or path, and sometimes we question why people do certain things or go down certain paths.

IF I GAVE YOU MY EYES

If I gave you my eyes you wouldn't like what you see, my heart can be so cold I question if it still belongs to me, every now and then I still catch an odd beat and that moment is when I feel complete.

The burden I carry upon my chest is much greater but I portray it to be less, I don't listen to the whispers or to the voices, I follow my gut and I make my own choices.

I'm accountable for my own wrongs, and I acknowledge my gains and a handful of friends is how the circle remains.

If I gave you my ears you couldn't process what I hear, and this is the reason it's hard to shed a tear, my mind is here, there, an everywhere and I'm dying of fear but I give the perception I don't really care.

I hide my feelings, I lock them up, and my bravado appears like I don't give a f*#k, but deep down I'm scared and highly confused and this has been the reason why I've stopped listening to the news.

I don't know what's fact from fiction, social media the new craze addiction we are all like fiends at the end of our phones all getting high of a Wi-Fi zone.

If I gave you my feet, you couldn't walk a day in my shoe's, so many choices do you win or do you lose, left or right, fight or flight and you have to make those decisions without hindsight.

WRITTEN BY
MR LISP

96

(This piece was inspired by my parents growing up I constantly use to hear my parents using phrases such as "Don't judge a book by its cover", "Still river's run deep" and "Don't trust everything you see as salt and sugar look the same" as I got older an obtained my own life experiences. I started to understand what my parents meant. We need to be less judgmental and have an overall understanding of others, treat people as individuals and try to understand that we are different with different morals, cultural backgrounds, life experience. Collectively these factors have an impact on how we process, interact, develop and the directions we take, so many times we believe we know someone, but do we know their story? We can see where we believe people are financially, socially, etc. Question do we know what they have been through to get to where they are? The choices and sacrifices that they had to make.)

Throughout life you will learn and understand you have to tell your story or someone else will tell it for you, let your story tell itself when you are no longer here and being laid to rest (unfortunately) how do you want to be remembered as they read your eulogy?

Your story should tell its own story, and you don't have to count on someone else to bullet point your life in 5 minutes you deserve more than that, while you have breath and blood running through your body, anything is possible and change can be made, you just have to be willing to decide how you want to be remembered.

Don't be who people tell you to be, be who you want to be in life. People are very good at dictating who they think you are or who you should be. Only you truly know who you are, even if you don't want to admit it or don't know how to truly release the inner you, it is there in you, and in due time and with personal development that character will be free.

YOUR STORY

You have to tell your story before someone tells it for you because you can't guarantee another person's point of view, will justify the true you.

Our past is our past, it can shape you greatly, but doesn't mean you can't be you, that doesn't mean you can't be true, it doesn't mean you have to remain in that skin, shed the excess, and repent for your sins, but don't forget to acknowledge and celebrate your well-deserved wins.

We live in the present that we get to unwrap and we have the ability to turn fiction into facts, talk less, action more, and keep ideas close to your chest, as your closest friend can still gossip with the rest.

Do what you want to do, please yourself, be the author of your own book, or the director of your own film, be what you want to be, have an impact and shape history, and let the next generation thrive off your legacy.

WRITTEN BY
MR LISP

(Do you believe your story currently reflects you to the max? If you were to unfortunately depart today, would you be happy with your story? This piece was written to stimulate and provoke your thought process, to get you to realise that life is short, do what makes you happy, be who you want to

be, and direct your story. If you want to be part of history, you have to make your own history, you're the only one who can decide how you want to be remembered and if you are remembered.)

CHOICE, CHANCE, CHANGE, in life you have to make the choice, to take a chance, if you want to make a change. We all have the power to make choices but how many of us will take the chance, to make a choice to obtain a goal, opportunities knock every day you just have to be willing to see them and embrace them.

THE 3 C'S OF LIFE

The three positive C's is something I believe, choice, change and chance, these three words can make your life advance.

You have to make a choice to change, level up, and get your frequency in range.

You may get a feeling that feels very strange, but go with your gut, the opportunity and chances won't leave you in a rut.

You have to take a chance to advance, what is there to lose? It's a simple decision, I know what I will choose, closed eyes keep you miles from the prize.

Fear, lack of self-confidence, and other people's lies, that's their issues, that's their night cries.

Give yourself the best opportunity, focus beyond what the eyes can see, let people tell you your goals are imaginary, can't be done, and show them you are more than someone's daughter or son, your ambitious, your

bold "you can and will" are the words that you were told.

WRITTEN BY
MR LISP

(Do you want change in your life? Do you want to take your chances? Do you make choices or allow others to make choices for you? This particular piece was written to highlight how important the three c's are to our lives and our personal development.)

This book is not a quick fix to your problems or issues it has been designed for you to pick up and reference at any time of your life/journey. You have been provided with some of the fundamental skills and techniques to really identify, learn and understand who you are, the skill sets for developing meaningful goals, and understanding why we sometimes fail (relapse and it is not the end of the world. It is definitely a learning opportunity.) Each skill requires understanding and development, as stated prior I recommend you read the spoken words/poetry more than once as there are some hidden gems strategically placed. As well as with personal development your mindset will change so you may relate differently to a piece now than you did originally. If you are willing to put the work in you will definitely reap the benefits, they say it takes you 30 days to create a habit but habits can change your life for the next 35 years. It may have taken you a few hours to read this book, but the knowledge you will keep and attain forever. It may take you 3-6 months to learn a new skill effectively but skills can really change your life.

Long-term thinking is fundamental: "slow progress is better than no progress." Believe in yourself and you will prevail to enormous heights.

I would personally like to say thank you for supporting me and I really hope that you have and will continue to find this book enjoyable and effective. I would love to hear, see and read your feedback, and hear about your personal developments, goals, success stories, etc.

Follow me @officialmrlisp feel free to comment, and share your thoughts and feedback.

PLEASE SCAN TO DOWNLOAD YOUR FREE RECOGNITION CERTIFICATE

Thank you for taking the time to read Recognition. I do hope you have found some of this information relevant, thought-provoking, self-motivating, and even life-changing.

MR LISP©

NOTES

NOTES

NOTES

NOTES

NOTES

Printed in Great Britain
by Amazon

86674013R00063